Seeing More Stars

Joseph Otterman

✸ Smithsonian

Consultants

Brian Mandell
Program Specialist
Smithsonian Science Education Center

Amy Zoque
STEM Coordinator and Instructional Coach
Vineyard STEM School
Ontario Montclair School District

Publishing Credits

Rachelle Cracchiolo, M.S.Ed., *Publisher*

Conni Medina, M.A.Ed., *Editor in Chief*

Diana Kenney, M.A.Ed., NBCT, *Series Developer*

Emily R. Smith, M.A.Ed., *Content Director*

Véronique Bos, *Creative Director*

Robin Erickson, *Art Director*

Michelle Jovin, M.A., *Associate Editor*

Mindy Duits, *Senior Graphic Designer*

Smithsonian Science Education Center

Image Credits: p.17 Jeremy Stanley/Flickr (Creative Commons); all other images from iStock and/or Shutterstock.

Library of Congress Cataloging-in-Publication Data

Names: Rice, Dona, author. | Smithsonian Institution.
Title: Seeing more stars / Dona Herweck Rice.
Description: Huntington Beach, CA : Teacher Created Materials, 2019. |
  Audience: K to grade 3. | Copyrighted 2020 by the Smithsonian
Institution.
  | Identifiers: LCCN 2018049795 (print) | LCCN 2018057687 (ebook) | ISBN
  9781493869008 (eBook) | ISBN 9781493866601 (pbk.)
Subjects: LCSH: Light pollution--Juvenile literature. | Exterior
  lighting--Juvenile literature. | Astronomy--Juvenile literature.
Classification: LCC QB51.3.L53 (ebook) | LCC QB51.3.L53 R53 2019 (print) |
  DDC 522--dc23
LC record available at https://lccn.loc.gov/2018049795

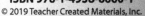

Smithsonian

Teacher Created Materials

5301 Oceanus Drive
Huntington Beach, CA 92649-1030
www.tcmpub.com
ISBN 978-1-4938-6660-1
© 2019 Teacher Created Materials, Inc.

Table of Contents

Star Bright

Star light, star bright, will I see a star tonight?

Light Pollution

Outdoor lights can block the light from stars. This is called *light pollution*. It can cause problems for most living things.

Dung beetles rely on a dark night sky to navigate.

Bright outdoor lights cause light pollution.

Some animals sleep during the day. They are awake at night. If there is too much light, they may not know it is nighttime!

A green sea turtle nests on a beach.

Turtle Trouble

Some sea turtles come to land at night to **nest**. They do not nest when there is too much light. No nests mean there will be no new turtles.

9

People need the dark to rest. Their bodies relax when the lights **dim**. People need the dark to sleep well too.

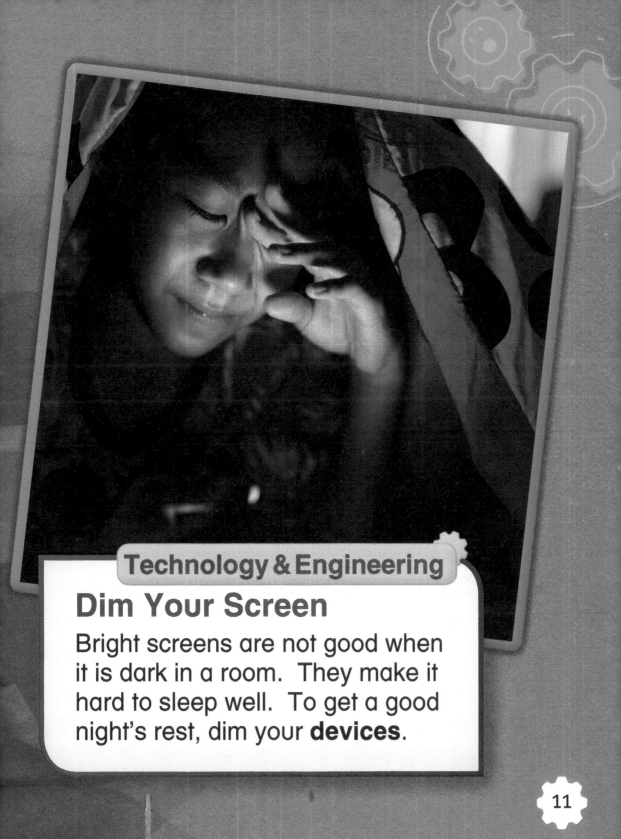

Dim Your Screen

Bright screens are not good when it is dark in a room. They make it hard to sleep well. To get a good night's rest, dim your **devices**.

A New Day

People want less light pollution. There is a lot they can do.

For one thing, people can turn off lights at night!

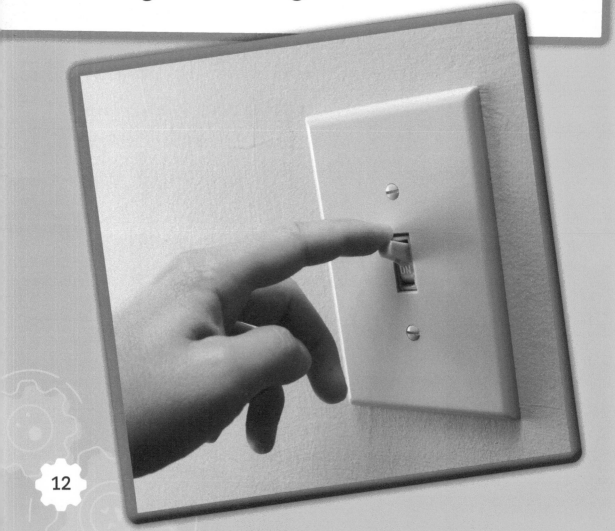

Next, people should look at all large outdoor lights. They should shine just where light is needed.

These lights only shine on the stairs.

These lights shine even where light is not needed.

Lastly, people should check the **brightness** of lights. Each light should shine just enough. Too much light is not helpful.

LED Lights

Choosing the wrong **LED lights** can be part of the problem. The hottest LED lights shine blue. These are good for daytime. Cooler LED lights shine yellow. These are right for nighttime.

the night sky with
no light pollution

the night sky with
light pollution

Lights Out

The sky without light pollution looks like a sea of stars. Maybe we will see more of them one day!

These backyard campers
can see a sky full of stars.

STEAM CHALLENGE

The Problem

You want to dim light pollution on your street. Your job is to stop extra light coming from streetlights. The streetlights must light the road but not the sky.

The Goals

- Create a hood for a streetlight that will focus the light.
- Create a hood using any material that will not burn when it is near a hot light bulb.
- Create a hood that can be tested on a table lamp.

1 Research and Brainstorm

What is the purpose of streetlights? How can you focus light?

2 Design and Build

Draw your plan. How will it work? What materials will you use? Build your hood!

3 Test and Improve

Place your model hood on a table lamp. Turn on the light. Does the light shine up? Does the light only shine down? Can you make it better? Try again.

4 Reflect and Share

How wide can you make the beam of light without the beam spreading? Would the hood help with light pollution?

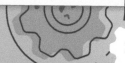

Glossary

brightness

devices

dim

LED lights

nest

Career Advice
from Smithsonian

Do you want to dim light pollution?
Here are some tips to get you started.

"Turn off lights at night to help dim light pollution. You will find it very rewarding!" *—Dr. Anne McDonough, Associate Director*

"Work hard in science, math, and engineering in school. And always think outside the box. You might just come up with an idea for dimming light pollution!" *—Dr. Brian Mandell, Division Director of Curriculum & Communications*